OPENING TO THE MYSTERY

Intimate
Spiritual Experiences
with My Daughter
That Cause Me
to Wonder

JAKE McARTHUR

SECOND EDITION

Second edition published in 2023/2024 by Kinetics Design, KDbooks.ca
ISBN 978-1-988360-90-4 (paperback)
ISBN 978-1-988360-91-1 (epub)

First edition published in 2019 by Kinetics Design, KDbooks.ca
Copyright © 2019 by Jake McArthur
ISBN 978-1-988360-29-4 (paperback)
ISBN 978-1-988360-30-0 (epub)

Editor: Eloise Lewis, LifeTales, www.lifetales.ca
Cover and interior design, typesetting and printing:
Daniel Crack, Kinetics Design, kdbooks.ca.
linkedin.com/in/kdbooks/

To Erica

My daughter, my teacher

MARCH 12, 1977 — AUGUST 30, 2000

Erica Lesley

March 12, 1977 - August 30, 2000

*I'll see you in the morning sun
and when the night is new
I'll be looking at the moon
but I'll be seeing you*

The quest for certainty blocks

the search for meaning.

— Eric Fromm

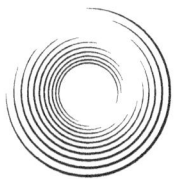

Try to love the questions themselves

as if they were locked rooms or books written

in a very foreign language.

Do not search for the answers,

which cannot be given to you now

because you would not be able to live them.

And the point is, to live everything.

Live the questions now.

— Rainer Maria Rilke

TABLE OF CONTENTS

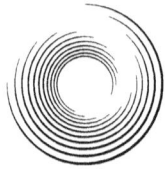

PREFACE

SINCE the original publication of *Opening to the Mystery* in 2019 I have had the pleasure of developing and performing a stage presentation of some of the stories and poems contained in the book. This has proven to be very satisfying for me and, based on feedback I've received, consistently impactful for audiences.

This year, 2023, is particularly poignant from my point of view. My daughter Erica was 23 years old when she died in a car accident on August 30, 2000 — twenty-three years ago.

This second edition of the book is being issued in honour of that fact. I have attempted to capture the poignancy of the timing with the following poem.

Twenty-Three

Twenty-three and twenty-three

Twenty-three years old
Twenty-three years ago

Incomprehensible and yet just understandable
if the mind squints and squishes time into
rational chapters marking a life …
arithmetic symmetry in a ragged reality.

When the car missed the turn
and found rock rather than future
her life was naively realized
packed full of
innocence and experience
joys and traumas
and love … I want to believe … love …

Dead as long as alive
the passage of years leaves now
frozen immature images and
pointless guesses about
possible choices and appearances
potential spirals of experience
dreams come true and
hearts broken …

Twenty-three and twenty-three
… eternity …
and life goes on.

JAKE MCARTHUR
August 30, 2023

To book a performance of Opening to the Mystery
Jake can be contacted at jakecelebrant@icloud.com.

INTRODUCTION

O N the morning of August 30, 2000, eight months after the end of my formal working career, I awoke, elated by the prospects of a new type of business venture I had launched the previous day. The events that followed in the next few hours shattered that elation and changed my life with an unimaginable profundity.

A knock on my door delivered news that no parent ever wants to hear: my daughter Erica, aged 23, had died in a car accident.

BEGINNINGS

I was thrilled beyond belief the day Erica was born, in 1977; thrilled that a baby girl was born out of what was a male-dominant gene pool (including her brother Colin, whose birth, two years earlier, had taken me to a state of unprecedented and overwhelming joy). As she grew, I was excited by her creativity and zest for living. I was also frustrated and often angered by many of her life decisions and behaviours during her short and dramatic life. And I have been variously inspired, heartbroken, relieved, and irreversibly transformed as a result of her death.

When Erica was five months old, her mother Nancy and I moved to England for an exciting job opportunity I had been offered. We lived there for a year before returning to Toronto. One day, when Erica was still less than a year old, she surprised us when she crawled into our bedroom, having escaped from the crib. Her irrepressible smile told us, "I did it!" That early persistent willfulness and zest for overcoming boundaries was a harbinger of what was to come during the balance of her life.

MY PURPOSE

I received a strong message several years ago via a medium that a piece of my life purpose was to use my person and my credibility to communicate about the possibilities hinted at in the stories to follow.

This book is a short selection of thoughts and stories about experiences I've had involving Erica. Some occurred while she was living on earth; some following her death.

The stories might be interpreted in a variety of ways. I've chosen to know them within the context of a loosely defined spirituality. To me, they reflect the possibility of a dimension of existence beyond, yet connected to, the material realm of my consciousness. In a sense, they feel mystical.

I acknowledge the possibility that I'm creating a self-reassuring story about Erica's continuing welfare. I also acknowledge that I may be simply and romantically rationalizing, in order to deny or mask my fear of a post-life nothingness. Years of discernment, periods of therapeutic support, and the experiences reflected herein have not supported those limiting assessments.

I profess no knowledge. I feel no certainty. I am curious — indeed, very curious — about what, if anything, might transpire after I expire. However, I feel no draw toward investing time in trying to understand what that might be. I simply wonder and revel in the mystery of it all. The experiences described in this book have led me further in my wondering, and wondering is the way I've chosen to carry on with my life.

I find the experiences fascinating and compelling — individually and even more in aggregate. That's enough to satisfy me. They lead me to wondering; and the openness that wondering partners with energizes my curiosity, my imagination, and my creativity.

My hope is that you will find the stories to be, at the very least, interesting. Perhaps they will in some way normalize your own experiences. Perhaps they will provide you with a desire to pursue your own journey of wondering. Perhaps they will challenge your own framing of such experiences and leave you upset, or angered, or open to new possibilities, or a combination of all.

Consider this my "coming out"!

Consider this your invitation to wonder about the mystery!

PART 1

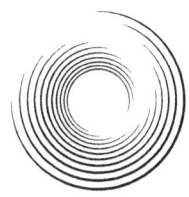

EXPERIENCES BEFORE ERICA's DEATH

———————

Life is not a problem to be solved,

but a reality to be experienced.

— SOREN KIERKEGAARD

———————

Soliloquy of Pain

IN November 1999, Erica called to say she wanted to get together for a conversation. She was married at the time. She told me she had been seeing a therapist and that she was finally ready to talk to me about her anger at my leaving her mother in 1987 when she had just recently turned 10. Of course I said, "Of course."

I'd been encouraging her to talk to me about that period; however, she always told me everything was okay and there was nothing to talk about. In view of her chaotic and adventurous, even dangerous, teen life, it seemed highly likely that there was much residue yet to be processed.

In early December, Erica drove over to our property in Caledon. By now I had remarried, and Roz and I had been living in the country since 1991. For over three hours, Erica poured out a perspective that I had never considered. When I left Nancy in 1987, Erica felt as if she'd lost her family — not simply that her father had left her mother. She clarified that I was the linchpin of the family for her; my absence meant the family no longer existed.

We shared many tears. I asked a few questions and I offered a few examples of where my recollection of events differed from hers, but chose to let her talk it out. And that's what she did. When she reached the end of her energy, I wrapped my arms around her and told her that I felt that I had completely heard her pain and sadness and the void she experienced. However, I didn't really feel any anger from her. She said that the anger had seemed to dissipate with the telling and being listened to. I told her this experience — her finally talking candidly about what had happened those years ago, from her 10-year-old point of view — was the greatest

Christmas gift I'd ever received. It was both heartbreaking and relieving. Little did I know how uncanny her timing would prove to be.

More than anything else, this conversation seemed to bring our relationship to a place of acceptance of what was, and what had been. For Erica, it seemed to be a significant letting-go of what she'd been carrying inside and consequently acting out for many years.

I don't believe in closure — the notion that something can be brought to an end — at least not when it comes to grieving. When it comes to losing someone you love, I prefer to think in terms of *integration*; at some point accepting and taking into yourself and your life the reality of what has occurred and allowing it to find a place within the body-mind-heart-spirit fibres of your being. Although I accepted Erica's truth about losing her family, my sense of personal responsibility for that pops up from time to time and I feel, once again, for a while, the pain of wrenching guilt.

This was the first of several experiences that, in hindsight, I interpret as preparations, on some energetic level, that were slowly unfolding for her pending departure.

I don't like to imagine how experiencing her loss would have transpired for me in the absence of that clarifying conversation.

COMING HOME

A short time after that conversation, Erica informed me that she had concluded her marriage wasn't, and wouldn't be, working and that she intended to leave it. I hadn't felt the marriage was a healthy one, so she didn't get much of a challenge from me. She asked if she could move in with Roz and me for "a couple of weeks" until she got herself sorted out. We agreed, and in the third week of January 2000, I helped her move.

Upon reflection, I find it interesting, perhaps even peculiar, but certainly synchronistic, that I had ended my working career the week before. So there we were, living under the same roof for the first time in many years, and neither of us had work commitments. As a result, we had the chance to spend significant time just hanging out, sharing leisurely breakfasts, and chatting over coffees.

After a few weeks (remember, it was only going to be a couple!), Erica concluded she wanted to study Early Childhood Education in the fall. As preparation, she took a job as a nanny for a family with four young children in a nearby village. She had always loved little kids and these ones were no exception. She also was fascinated with their mother who provided massage, yoga, and other healing modalities from her studio in their home. Erica quickly became enthralled with the spirituality that this woman spoke of and practiced.

Now with more time to connect with the forest and fields on our property, I began to more fully experience a strong sense that there was more going on in the reality of the make-up of the property than I had previously been conscious of. I didn't understand it; however, I became open to the possibility that there might be another dimension of existence that hadn't made itself apparent until then. In a lovely synchronicity

I discovered the book *The Web of Life* by physicist Fritjof Capra. It laid the groundwork for my own framing and experiencing of the connectedness of all existence, and ultimately set off a deep and passionate exploration that focused on experiencing and internalizing spirituality in my daily living.

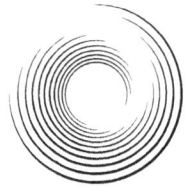

CONVERSATIONS WITH GOD

IN March 2000, a friend, Bob, who is a management consultant, suggested we get together to discuss a new concept he was developing that might interest me. He agreed to drive out to the country where we lived, and as we had lunch, he described what he had in mind.

As lunch came to an end, he asked if I had read the book *Conversations with God*. I replied that I'd seen the book in bookstores but really thought nothing of it. The title had struck me as contrived and presumptuous and so I had judged it as "not for me." He went on to describe how he and his brother had found the book incredibly stimulating and thought-provoking. So I made a mental note to perhaps reconsider my initial opinion. He did add that he had also gone to hear the author, Neale Donald Walsh, and had come away completely unimpressed and questioning his sincerity.

As Bob was getting ready to leave, Erica returned home from her workday. We all spoke for a few minutes and then I walked Bob to his car. I came back into the house to find Erica sprawled sideways across a mammoth chair out in the sunroom. She had a wide grin and look of great satisfaction on her face. I sat down and commented that she sure looked happy. I said, "So tell me, what's up that's making you so happy?" She related how much she was loving her role as a nanny (she had had one when she was young) and how much she loved working for Millie, the mother of the family. Millie was sharing much of her insight into yoga and spirituality and Erica was revelling in that. She went on to say that just as she was leaving for home, Millie came to her and told her she had two copies of a particular book. She couldn't remember why she had two copies or how she came to have them, but that now she knew one of the copies was intended for Erica. I asked what the title of the book was and, sure enough, it was *Conversations with God*. I told Erica about my "conversation with Bob" and we both concluded that something must be up. We committed to read the book and share our thoughts about it.

I found the book more interesting than I thought I would. Around the time we both finished reading it, I discovered that the author was giving an evening talk in the town of Fergus, about an hour away from our home. Erica and I resolved to attend. We had a lovely drive there, shared a light meal, and secured seats right at the front of the hall. We had the same reaction that Bob had described. Neale Donald Walsh came across as a flimflam man. He seemed extremely insincere and significantly full of himself.

And yet, the book had some inexplicable resonance and the coincidence (synchronicity!) of our both hearing about the book the same day held our attention, even if the author did not.

Before too long, the book faded into the background as Erica and I shared other spiritual experiences. I had forgotten this story until I sat down to create this book.

Near-Death Experience Story
and the Healing Cabin

IN the spring of 2000, Erica and I attended a talk, in a barn in the nearby town of Bolton, that Erica's employer had told her about. A woman named Shirley, who had had a near-death experience, gave the talk. She expressed her shyness and explained she had never spoken publicly about this experience, but for some reason she didn't understand, she now felt compelled to do so. Due to her lack of confidence, she had prerecorded an audio of her presentation.

It was difficult to hear clearly because of the quality of the recording; however, each of us, in our own way, was captivated by the story. I don't remember the specific details and actually, since then, I've read about so many near-death experiences that they've all melded together. What I do recall in listening to, and in subsequently speaking with, Shirley, was her utter lack of guile or pretension. She felt completely sincere to me then and that feeling has never wavered. I had never listened to someone tell their near-death story. At the time it was interesting. In retrospect, it was curious timing.

Erica and I later spoke with Shirley and she invited us to visit her at her property near Napanee, Ontario. She and her husband had discovered a large quartz deposit on the property and he had built a cabin over the deposit. Erica and I took Shirley up on the offer in April.

On the property, we each experienced a guided meditation while floating on a raft in a small pool inside the healing cabin. This was still in the early stages of my spiritual journey and I wasn't comfortable giving myself over to the recorded guiding. However, it was peaceful.

Before we left, Shirley gave Erica a small, carved wooden turtle necklace on a rawhide cord. She explained that a Native Canadian chief had given several of these to her, suggesting she give them to young people she might meet when she thought it was appropriate. She believed Erica was an appropriate choice. When I later called Shirley to tell her of Erica's death, her first question was to ask if Erica had been wearing the turtle. I explained she wasn't and that it was the first thing I had noticed in her room when I went in after her accident. I wore that necklace for several years.

Erica had returned to the healing cabin a few weeks later to join with a number of spiritual mediums. Among other experiences she had that weekend was a past life regression in which she was told she had lived in France during WWII and had fallen in love with a pilot whose plane had been shot down. I don't recall any other details. This story has a connection with a further story later in the book, *I'm Thinking of You*.

HOSPICE AND RAINBOWS

FOR several years I had a vague knowledge of the hospice movement. I had a friend who was the chairman of the hospice organization in Ontario. However, I had never clearly understood what hospice was about. As I entered into my new unemployed life I decided to get involved in some not-for-profit activity, and hospice came to mind. Having studied its website, I got in touch with Hospice Caledon and discovered there was a volunteer training program about to commence. I took the training, which was primarily focused on palliative care support, and, with some degree of trepidation, looked forward to beginning that experience.

As the hospice training was coming to completion in the spring, I discovered that hospice also sponsored a child bereavement program called Rainbows and concluded it would also be of interest to me. Interestingly, there was a Rainbows training program just about to begin and I took that training as well. When I described that to Erica, she became very interested and exclaimed how cool it would be for us to deliver Rainbows programs together. I agreed. Of course, we never got to do that.

When Erica's accident occurred, shortly after I had completed my training, I was told I'd have to wait at least a year before I could begin actually volunteering in either hospice or Rainbows activities. I didn't understand this at the time, as I thought I was doing fine. Only later did I realize how important it was that I do work on my own healing journey before endeavouring to support others.

I did eventually facilitate Rainbows groups at a local elementary school for several years and I became involved in a variety of volunteer activities at several hospices. Those activities included: sitting with clients receiving palliative care; facilitating bereavement groups for adults as well as groups for children; training new volunteers about the spiritual dimensions of providing care; training staff about leadership; leading poetry workshops; using poetry as a means of expression around dying and grieving; writing poetry for hospice events; and writing and leading group rituals around remembering loved ones who have died.

As I look back, it seems very curious that I took both of those training programs during the months prior to Erica's death. It's impossible for me to express how valuable the training was in terms of contributing to my comfort levels, such as they were, in the early days following the accident. Over the years, that connection has provided such rich experiences and such poignant opportunities to honour Erica and to continue my own healing journey.

SUMMER 2000

THE summer of 2000 was characterized by some dramatic family experiences.

With great energy and excitement, Erica helped me plan and arrange a 50th birthday party for Roz at our property in Caledon. She told me she was tingling with excitement at the prospect of acknowledging and celebrating this woman who had so generously and lovingly embraced her.

Shortly after that, my son Colin and I travelled to the Yukon and, over four days, hiked the Chilkoot Trail, which runs from Skagway, Alaska, over the Chilkoot Pass into Northern British Columbia. This was one of the routes that seekers of gold had followed to get to the Klondike Gold Rush near Dawson City, Yukon. It was a remarkable experience not just for the physical experience of hiking and climbing but, more importantly, for the strong bonding experience Colin and I shared.

Early in August, Erica was visiting Colin at his apartment when their mother Nancy called to speak with Colin. He told her Erica was there and asked if she'd like to speak with her. They did speak and arranged to get together for dinner a couple of weeks later. The day came, and with a certain amount of trepidation, Erica drove into Toronto for the dinner. I say trepidation because for many years Erica had had a challenging relationship with her mom and went significant periods of time without seeing her.

I wasn't home when she left and she didn't come back until the next day. I'll never forget the moment I poked my head through the door into the TV room and asked her how the evening had gone. A magnificent smile broke out across her face and she exclaimed that it had been the greatest time. She related some of the things they had spoken about and then poignantly said that, for the first time, she felt that her mother just accepted her for who she was and wasn't disappointed that she wasn't some perhaps more preferred version of a daughter, and she loved her just the way she was. Erica was ecstatic; I felt delighted for her and pleased for Nancy that they were possibly entering a new stage of their relationship.

In the past, when they got together, frequent arguments and unkind words kicked off another period of estrangement. So it seems timely beyond coincidence that this lovely evening transpired only a couple of weeks before Erica's accident.

THE PIVOTAL EXPERIENCE

THE last week of August, Erica went to a vacation resort with the family whose children she was caring for, as preparation for her return to school to study Early Childhood Education. Indelibly, both Roz and I recall her bouncy farewell, with hugs, kisses, and "I love you's", and her cosmic smile beaming through her car window as she drove off.

On August 29, I had been showcasing a new coaching/facilitation venture I was about to start up. After the event, I drove my best friend home and, sitting in the car outside his house, remarked that I was so excited and delighted with how my life was flowing and with how Erica seemed to be finally getting her life together. I returned home that night elated, eagerly wanting to share with Roz the excitement of the positive reception. She was asleep, so, with the wisdom accumulated from our years together, I waited until morning.

On the way downstairs for breakfast before launching into my story, Roz told me matter-of-factly that Gilly, one of our black labs, had run off the night before and I made a mental note that we'd have to round him up later on. Gilly had run away from our property numerous times to his favourite, though varied, target hangouts. Not once had he managed to find his way home. I was therefore shocked when I looked outside the kitchen door and saw Gilly calmly walking across the parking area toward the house. I mused that he had obviously gotten lost within his frame of reference and to his surprise discovered he was home. I was later prompted to focus on this episode as one of the ways I chose to spiritually frame the subsequent events of that day. The poem on page 28, *The Ballad of Gilly*, reflects an attempt at some relative levity.

Around 8:30, as we were finishing breakfast and I had just about finished recounting the joy of the previous evening, there was a knock on the kitchen door, which was somewhat unusual, given the seclusion of where we lived and the length of the driveway. Outside was a police officer who, upon confirming my identity, asked to come in. He suggested we sit down.

In a calm, carefully paced and pitched voice, he gently and compassionately informed us there had been a car accident; that it had been a serious accident; that Erica had been involved in the accident and that she hadn't survived. Time stopped, the world tilted, and as the words "… hadn't survived" crept piercingly into my consciousness, an agonizing silent scream erupted and flowed out of me in molten tears, quivering body and quavering primal sounds … until my "manly" self reasserted control. The officer indicated someone would have to go the hospital to identify Erica and, on the basis that we wouldn't want this to be our final and lasting image of her, strongly suggested we have a family member or friend go. Roz and I looked at each other and instantly confirmed that we would go ourselves.

We found out subsequently that Erica had been given the night off by the family and had gone out partying with some friends. They had wisely taken cabs into Barrie from the nearby resort. Somehow, later that night, Erica had ultimately returned to the resort and gotten into her car with a young man she'd met. The accident occurred two minutes from the resort. Neither of them survived.

After an hour of driving to the hospital, amid tears and trauma-induced laughter, recalling some of the humorous incidents in Erica's life, we sat what seemed an interminably long time in a hospital waiting room until we were directed to follow a staff member through a closed door. From the doorway, I could see a gurney, angled toward the back right corner of the hospital-green painted room. A white sheet covered a body. An attendant had pulled back the sheet, exposing the head and an expressionless face. On reluctant, rubbery legs, I moved closer, and I believe the words, "Yes, that's her," fell lifelessly from my tongue. And yet … as those words were spoken, I was filled and embraced with the certain, unshakeable clarity that in fact it wasn't her. Yes, it was the package she came in during her 23-year life, but she, the essence of Erica, the spirit of my daughter, in fact was clearly not there. In fractions of a nanosecond, without thinking about it, without analysis, and without rationale, I knew that her soul had left. It had moved on, alive in whatever way a soul lives in non-incarnated form, having left in dead form the body I had associated with her.

This was a transforming moment in my life, a transforming moment in my spiritual awakening, and a transforming moment in my relationship with death and dying. It was a primordial letting be and letting go. It was an instant of certainty in a broader story where I otherwise feel no certainty.

I know it could be argued that what I've described was a neat and tidy form of pain-managing denial, perhaps just a story I told myself in order to alleviate the suffering of an incomprehensible loss. And in one sense, that might be accurate. For a period of several months, I chose to experience Erica's death in this comforting spiritual cocoon until, eventually, unable to continue the fabrication of comfort, I faced up to the depth, the wrenching, and the anguish of my loss of her physical presence in my life and in the lives of others who loved her.

That grieving process continues to this day, and I believe it will continue the rest of my life. In fact, I want my grief to continue. I don't ever want to live without that palpable scar of loss. However, I never did have a sense of grieving on her behalf. The certainty I felt in that moment of viewing her lifeless body that the real "she" had simply moved on, not died, has never wavered over the years that have followed. In tandem with that realization, I have an abiding sense of Erica's presence continuing in my life. I use the word realization rather than feeling, because in all of my discernment about that experience there resides a simple and clear *isness* that doesn't require further explanation or elaboration. While obviously I have memories and feelings and thoughts and the residual of lessons that I learned from her, I also have a sense of her real presence in some proximal yet ineffable relationship that informs my being and my living to this day.

The Ballad of Gilly

Oh where did you come from Gilly my boy
Oh how did you make your way home
Were you confused, did you get turned around
You've never returned when you've roamed.

Oh how was it this morning Gilly my boy
This day of all days you came back
With she who best loved you forever gone
What mysterious hand got you on track.

Oh I've an idea goofy Gilly my boy
Of how you got home on this day
She guided you here to save your black hide
With a message for us — "all's OK."

Oh perhaps that's the truth Gilly my boy
Though a young one with wisdom opined
That we had enough on our plate for one day
So her spirit helped you settle our mind.

So now she's gone and you're here Gilly boy
A bargain I'd never have made
Yet your presence reflects her compassion
That's the best we're left now I'm afraid.

PART 2

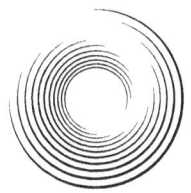

EXPERIENCES AFTER
ERICA'S DEATH

———————

Truly, we live with mysteries too marvelous

to be understood …

Let me keep my distance, always, from those

who think they have the answers.

Let me keep company always with those who say

"Look!" and laugh in astonishment,

and bow their heads.

— MARY OLIVER, FROM *Mysteries, Yes*

———————

A SCENT BEYOND ROSES

IN the days that followed the accident, I was very clear that I didn't want to visit the accident site. I convinced myself that there could be no value in that. In retrospect, I suspect I was really avoiding the imagined pain and perhaps overwhelming devastation of being in that place.

In any event, I woke up one Saturday in late October and had a strong urge for the first time to make that journey. It was about an hour from our home, and Roz wanted to come with me, so we set out, not quite certain about the exact location, but knowing the road. We confirmed the location from the proprietor of a convenience store, who was aware of the accident. Fitting the description the police had given us, the road driving from the east came down a steep hill and went into a sharp curve. It was this turn that Erica had missed. Her car, continuing straight, had come to a jolting end in a small rock-strewn field.

When we arrived at the spot, we pulled into a dirt lane right beside that field. Feeling a mixture of reluctance and attraction, we got out of the car and walked through a small copse of trees. As we passed the last tree and entered the field, not conscious of what we might be expecting, each of us, at exactly the same time, was engulfed in an indescribable floral-like scent. We were filled with it until we could no longer discern it. The scent was powerful and richly exotic, however, we couldn't identify it. Rationally, we began searching for the source. However, in late October in Ontario, there is no flowering or otherwise scented greenery. As we searched, we came across the VW insignia that had been on the front of Erica's Volkswagen Jetta.

As tears flowed, we came to the conclusion that the only possible explanation of the scent was that it must have been somehow spiritually induced. We interpreted the message as a sign that "All is well"— perhaps even that "All is beautiful … beyond what you can know or even imagine." It felt reassuring. And, of course, it might have been another necessary means of dealing with the grief. Or not …

I hadn't come across any other stories of grieving people having this experience. Then, a few years later, as a hospice volunteer, I was visiting with a mother whose 22-year-old son had died in a motorcycle accident. We sat in her kitchen over coffee. Naturally, she was distraught, and our conversation of a couple of hours was focused on her tearful descriptions of her son and memories of his life. Toward the end, she said that she'd had another experience but that I'd think she was crazy if she told it. I said that there are no crazy stories and that I'd love to hear it if she wanted to tell me. Similar to my original feeling, she hadn't wanted to visit the site of her son's accident. Finally, the day came when she changed her mind. Her husband didn't want to go, so her sister joined her. When they arrived at the location and stepped out of the car, they each were filled with an indescribable scent … a scent she could only say was "beyond roses." I related my experience and we shared some tears. And we both knew that if the story was crazy … well then, we were both crazy! I was pretty sure neither of us was.

I'm Thinking of You

ON a late, clear autumn afternoon in October 2003, I was warming the barbeque for dinner. With a glass of red wine in my hand, I had sat down on the edge of the deck with my eleven-year-old black lab, Buddy. Ruffling his hair, as his head rested on his forelegs, I gazed over toward the old white ash, almost denuded of leaves, and thought about our Rottweiler, Marley, whom we had put down, due to cancer, under that tree, several weeks earlier. Still wincing a bit from that loss, I mused quietly to Buddy that it had been a while since we had seen Marley. With that, his head shot straight up, his ears pricked up, and he looked out for her. With my *superior human wisdom*, I smiled and scratched his head, and assured him that Marley wasn't there, that I was just thinking about her.

A few moments later, I was looking out toward the blue spruce, as I did frequently, which had been planted by friends in memory of Erica. As I was thinking about Erica, I again mused out loud that it had been a very long time since we had seen Erica. Instantly, Buddy's head shot up again, his ears pricked up and he began looking around. Again, I assured him Erica wasn't there. Or so I thought.

I had no sooner spoken those words, than a musical phrase came into my head: "I'm thinking of you at this moment; of you at this moment I'm thinking of you ..." with a clear tune that I remember labelling as a 1940s wartime sound, with a feeling that a violin and an accordion were providing instrumental accompaniment. I say it came into my head; in fact, it was as if my entire being was both filled with and engulfed in that musical phrase. And it didn't leave. All through that evening, the words and unchanging tune continued to surface in my consciousness. It continued as I was going to sleep and was on my lips as I awoke the next morning. It was still there on the trail as I was walking my dogs, and new lyrics began flowing.

I am a poet and I do very often receive inspiration when I'm in the midst of nature, often when walking these trails. However, these arriving messages weren't simply poetic; they were clearly musical lyrics and I had an unshakeable sense that I should pay close attention to them, although, at the same time, I also had a strong sense that lasted for several weeks that I wasn't to write them down. That, in itself, was, and is, interesting to me because usually when a poetic riff hits me, I get it down as soon as possible, fearing it will drift into the ether. I had none of that fear in this instance. As the days continued, lyric phrases continued to flow into my consciousness.

Finally, on November 5, I was working outside in the yard when I was clearly prompted or compelled to go to my office and write down the lyrics, which I did.

A few months later, I sang the song for a brother-in-law as a prelude to recording it. He's a musician and he immediately reflected that it sounded like a French waltz. That struck a chord, so to speak. Only then did I recall that Erica had spent that weekend in June 2000 at a gathering of mediums and other new age practitioners. On her return, she had told me she had experienced a past life regression indicating she had been living in France during World War II and had had a relationship with an air force pilot of unknown nationality. As an interesting aside, I subsequently recalled that I had an uncle who had been an RCAF pilot during that war and had been shot down and disappeared, presumed dead, flying a mission over Germany. That struck me as an interesting coincidence!

The song has been one of the most wonderful blessings I've received on this journey. The lyrics follow.

I'm Thinking of You

I'm thinking of you
At this moment
Of you
In this moment
I'm thinking of you

I'm dreaming of you
At this moment
Of you
In this moment
This dream seems so true

I'm dancing with you
At this moment
Holding you
In this moment
We're dancing we two

Sometimes
I catch myself sighing
Feel myself crying
'Cause I'm missing you
Sometimes
I'm joyfully singing
Bells seem to be ringing
Singing and ringing
The song that is you

I'm smiling at you
At this moment
With you
In this moment
I'm smiling with you

I'm laughing at you
In this moment
With you
At this moment
I'm laughing with you

Your laughter and smile
At this moment
For a while
In this moment
Warm me through and through

Sometimes
I catch myself sighing
Unexpectedly crying
'Cause I'm missing you
Sometimes
I'm wistfully singing
Bells seem to be ringing
Singing and ringing
A song just for you

I'm being with you
At this moment
Once again
In this moment
I'm being with you

Then, I'm angry with you
At this moment
This won't do
In this moment
This not having you

Yet, you're here in my heart
At this moment
This love
Every moment
Remains in my heart

Sometimes
I catch myself sighing
Uncontrollably crying
'Cause I'm missing you
Sometimes
I'm joyfully singing
Bells seem to be ringing
I hear your voice singing
Singing and ringing
The song that is you

So … I'm
Thinking and smiling
Laughing and singing
Sighing and crying
Dancing and ringing
Missing and loving
Clear then confusing
Apart still together
Sad yet amusing

Yes …
I have these memories
Here in my heart
Now and forever
… of you.

VISITATION

IN the summer of 2006, Roz and I were at a weekend retreat with her family at a cottage on a flooded portion of the Ottawa River in Northern Ontario. One beautiful sun-filled morning I was heading out for a paddle with a nephew when his father called him to say he'd have to leave with him now if he wanted to get a fishing licence. While I was looking forward to the experience with Dylan, I was also happy to spend some time on the water alone.

As I paddled out on the quiet water, I felt that the human world seemed to disappear and I was enveloped in peace and stillness, as the quiet strokes of the paddle propelled me into a series of small dead-end bays. What then transpired was thrilling. I can feel the total captivation yet again as I'm writing these words. The experience involved an extended, intimate interaction with a monarch butterfly; it lasted at least 30 minutes. I've spent a lot of time outdoors in my life, and I've seen many monarch butterflies. To have this being flutter around me, and land, and rest on various parts of my body and face over that length of time was simply extraordinary. Reflecting back, I recall that in the immediate weeks following Erica's accident, numerous monarch butterflies just showed up seemingly out of nowhere. I have my own mystical sense of what these presences are about. In conversation with others, I have heard frequently of visitations and interactions with deer, dragonflies, birds, and other natural beings in the days following the death of a loved one.

Later that day, I began to write a narrative poem about that experience. The writing gave me an opportunity to capture and articulate the senses of awe, mystery, and gratitude I was feeling. I've loved having opportunities to read this poem to others and to engage in rich conversation about the possible messages it carries.

Visitation

On a sun-bathed
August Sunday morning
my green canoe slips easily
through the still water
in the silent, narrowing
low-banked bay.

Otter slides off the right bank
and glides intentionally,
apparently care-free,
directly toward the
stern-turned-bow
and in an instant before
possible collision
Dips effortlessly
twists purposefully
and passes by me
inches below the surface.
Later, he returns from
the opposite bank
head obscured
mouth bulging
with lime-green foliage salad.

Before his reappearance
my awareness falls on your
    appearance
floating, flitting, flowing
bobbing, turning, sweeping
on glorious wings
circling the canoe
circling me
in sight
out of sight
in sight again
you settle on the bow rope
wings breathing peacefully
orange and black and white
our hearts beat

and I breathe
trying to synchronize with
the rhythm of your wings.

And the canoe floats aimlessly
gently bumps a bank
as I smile
at you and with you
my hands leaning on the paddle
cross the gunnels
and you're away
hovering again around the canoe.
I sense you unseen on my
    right shoulder
and you come to rest on my
    right hand
I strain to feel
your weightless weight
supported on two-toed slender
    black stilts.
You appear so trusting
wings breathing easily
as your proboscis
grazes the salt-mine pores
stirring up tiny silver bursts
    of light.

I journey and sip
the broad geography of your wings
irregular orange fields
bordered by black hedge rows,
white bleeding from the edges
as they open and close
open and close
in silent moving meditation.
I slowly raise the paddle
and ever so gently propel along
    the bank
and you don't stir

as the paddle crosses
left, back right and dips into
    the water
you languish intentionally
apparently certain you're safe
secure in the aura
of the salt lick.

Then, away again
you circle and
you land on my right ear.
I feel now your gripping;
you're holding tight
you have my attention
I listen for a message
'I'm here and there
I'm everywhere and nowhere
always and never
in and out of form' ...
and the message feels like
    an erotic kiss
as you continue your
    delicate buffet.

And away again
you flutter

and you find a way to take hold
on my right cheek
just below my eye.

And I begin to cry with joy
at this uncommon intimacy
in this moment
and you feast on my tears
as I feast on your presence.
And I continue a meditative stroke.

We leave the bay
and cross out into open water
and you stay with me.

Breeze is up in the bright
    noon sun
and still you stay with me
kissing my cheek
caressing my nose and eye
with your breathing wings ...
I'm sighing and gasping
that you stay even still
seeming so effortless
seeming so certain
seeming so trusting
seeming so loving.

And then ...
as I become aware of the
    approaching shore
I ask you to stay
so I can share your visit with
    the others.
And in the instant
the spell is broken
as I yearn for your
ever-presence
you disengage from our
    intimate dance
your purpose apparently served.
Once more around the canoe
    you hover
and you're gone ...
for now
in this moment
in this form.

And I'm filled with gratitude
and I'm bathed in love
and I accept
with awe and wonder
the mystery of
your visit.

Dream Time — Waking Time
— Healing

O N the morning of May 3, 2005, nearly five years after Erica's accident, I awoke around 3:30 and felt instantly alert. I was filled with a sense that something important had just happened. As I lay listening, in the silence, for any sounds that might have been connected to this sense of alertness, I realized I was filled with the images and memory of an experience I had just encountered. I felt myself open to the contents of a dream. It wasn't that I rewound the reel and relived it. I simply, somehow, felt myself infused with images and feelings and thoughts and dialogue of a sort that combined in a powerful resonating presence.

In preparation for a pending intensive session in the Doctor of Ministry program, where the Art as Meditation segment was to be led by Jeremy Taylor, I had read his book *When People Fly and Water Runs Uphill*. It described the value in journaling dreams and doing so immediately upon waking, ideally with only minimal movement, in order to most effectively recall details accurately. This morning, for some reason, I was transfixed and simply lay in bed filled with this dream experience, being with it and connecting it to an earlier experience in my waking life.

In the dream, I am in a hazily outlined room with a greenish aura. There is no definition to the peripheral space and my visual attention is riveted on a gurney that is situated to my left angling toward the back right corner. The rest of the room is very vague and veiled, with no other physical detail apparent. I have a sense of presences in the room; however, I see no one.

On the gurney lies a female body, naked from the waist up. In the dream, I am certain that the body is dead. I have the strong sense the body is that of my daughter, Erica, although at no time during the dream do I actually see her face. One of the presences (a doctor? a nurse?) seems to apply a clear liquid to a small, approximately one-inch incision on the outside of the left breast, at the base. While I don't hear a voice speaking, I receive a clear message instructing me to blow on the liquid in order to dry it. I draw back and hesitate. Without speaking, I somehow communicate a response that this is my daughter and I can't get that intimately close to her breast. However, I receive a message back that it is important that I do this. I consider this and then move closer, bend over the body and blow gently on the incision. With that, I awake.

At the dream-work intensive, I was blessed to have the opportunity to participate in a small group of students sharing our dreams. Just as it came to my turn, Jeremy Taylor joined us as he was moving between the groups. I consider that a fascinating synchronicity, given the importance I view the dream having in my life. Using Taylor's methodology, others reflected on the dream using the introductory phrase, *If this were my dream …*

The observations included:

- The notion that the Breath of Life/Breath of the Divine was within me.

- Given the left breast is proximal to the heart, there is a sense of tenderness and gentleness.

- It's very rare in a dream that someone changes his mind. This speaks to how important it was to do what I did.

- The lack of faces, my own comfort and acceptance of the restricted peripheral vision, and my acceptance of the dramatic focus (the body on the gurney) together suggest that this was a big archetypal moment. While it includes the sense of my own healing and of Erica's healing, it speaks on a transpersonal level to healing even bigger wounds.

- The absence of speech and sound, only sensing communication, points to perhaps the invitation to step up to more clearly speaking truth and/or to celebrate an innate ability/gift to heal (perhaps healing women or mother earth, or facilitating access for men to the divine feminine and/or their own animus).

- Many ancient religions believed the living had a responsibility to pray for the dead. Perhaps the dream reflects a call to pray for healing of residual wounds of my daughter. As I'm writing this, I also wonder whether it might be a call to do the same for my deceased father who had imposed some emotional and physical wounds on me.

- Interestingly, three of the five women in the group had experienced breast biopsies, and all confirmed that the incision they experienced was in the same place and of the same length as the one in my dream.

During that intensive, Taylor stated that all dreams come in the service of moving toward health and wholeness, related on one or more levels to the individual, the human species, the biosphere, and the cosmos. He also indicated that the stronger the denial of a suggested interpretation arising from a dream projection process, the greater the likelihood of its being close to the mark.

At the time of the dream work experience, I had a particularly difficult time accepting the notion that I had some kind of healing capability and so initially downplayed that interpretive possibility. However, another Wisdom University resource and friend, the late John Parente, gave me a framing that fit far more comfortably: we are not healers of another; rather, we may facilitate others' healing of themselves. That was enriched even further for me with the framing, put forth by teachers Judith Yost and Will Taegel, that we can experience and assist in transformation as opposed to healing.

Of course, the image of the body on the gurney reprised my memory of the experience of identifying Erica in the hospital. It stunned me that the unconscious had retained that image so vividly and that it shook loose and emerged when it did. The following poem speaks to the integration of the two experiences.

Dream Time — Waking Time — Healing

Faceless image emerges from the deep vault in a
necessary dream through a green mist

in a green room and merges with waking reality through the grey fog
of my conscious dreamlike memory.

The naked body, unclaimed meat, lies cold and rigid on the gunmetal grey
gurney — mortal intimacy deepening the bone-chilling ache in my bones.

Urged healing breath toward the salved surgical slit on her left
breast — exhalation for wholeness — slips through the lips

that kissed the lifeless forehead final goodbye.

Required identification elicits an essential revelation of soul-full,
soul-less realities.

A certainty of passage unwraps the balming mummification
from the decaying remains of my attachment.

Will the lessons of grief ever end?

I don't know, with certainty, how dreams arise and from where the content is sourced. I am certain, however, that the dream, the time sharing and assessing it, and the experience of reflection all provide a mysterious and powerful connection to Erica. Writing this poem and combining the reflections on both the real event and the dream allowed me to travel deeper into the moments of revelation. The rawness and bareness of the expression provided a clarity of meaning for me from each of the experiences.

Rabbit and Coyote

ON the sunlit wintry morning of January 25, 2007, I was walking my dogs and we came upon the fresh remains of a of a rabbit hunted by a coyote. Its red blood seemed alive and somehow still oxygenated, and the fur, with its beiges, browns, and whites, had a fluffed, fresh appearance. I was taken by the primal beauty while also having a romantic sense of the heartbeats, the fear, and the hunger that would have characterized the food chain dance.

Later that day, I wrote a poem I called *Living Blood* which primarily captured the awe of the image and the experience. Five days later, I had a dream in which I was trying to parallel park my vehicle along the grassy shoulder of a country road. I kept seeing many decaying rabbit pelts strewn on the shoulder and I kept backing up my car trying to find a spot to park where I wouldn't have to step on one of them. I woke before I succeeded. The experience of the dream caused me to challenge my mystical romantic relationship with nature, which, in turn, led me to revisit the earlier experience and write a second poem, *Living Blood: Revisited*, which took into account the visceral reality of the kill.

In the process of writing that second poem I became conscious of a rising connection to Erica. I ultimately realized that, while I had visited the site of her accident, I had never chosen to allow myself to imagine the horror of those final moments of her life. I shivered just thinking about the idea of doing that. However, the following day I sat down and, grounded through a deep meditation, wrote what my imagination would allow to come forth.

And so, six and a half years after her death, I felt I had finally been able to allow myself to dive into the reality of her dying. It wasn't like I was consciously avoiding that; however, I was undoubtedly avoiding the imaginary experience of the moments of the accident.

Somehow, circumstances were such that I was awoken to confront the horror of her tragedy. In retrospect, it feels as if that was something I needed to face and then let go of. The student was ready and the teacher appeared.

The complete *Living Blood Trilogy* can be found in Appendix II. Here is the final poem of the trilogy:

Living Blood: A Finally-Opened Sore

I can hear your wild laughter
bursting forth as you begin,
in the shadow of prudent travel,
the ill-advised adventure
to who knows where.

I can hear your gasp of incredulity
brainstem flashing primordial warning
as the curve is missed
and you veer off the road
into the dark void.

I can hear your scream!
I can hear your scream!
I can hear your scream!
I can hear your scream!

piercing the seconds to eternity
as excitement crashes into chaos
as the car violently leaps and careens
against and over the unseen boulders.

I can feel the smashing of hard metal
against the softness of your defenceless body
crushing and ripping your corporal being
drenching the world in the blood of your living.

The laws of physics and forces
viciously declaring their truth
strangling your laughter
erasing your smile
throwing you free of the mutilating machine
throwing you free of the bonds of mortality.

Oh God!
For so long I've avoided
this intimacy with your destruction.
For so long I've hidden out
in the metal-free meadows of illusion.
Swaddling myself in the beautiful memories,
wrapping my fear and ache in the tissue paper of spirit.
Lacking the courage to really smell your fear.
Lacking the courage to view the imagined video.
Lacking the courage to remove the earplugs from my heart
and really hear
and really hear
the horror
of your scream,
the mangling of metal
the grinding of rock
the tearing of grasses.

This day, in this visceral rawness
of my unpackaged vulnerability,
opened to the reality of your dying,
freed to the starkness of your fear,
choking on the loneliness of your suffering,
angry at your disregard of reality,
emptied of the meaning of your sacrifice —
Closer to the scream in my heart
sinking in the sadness
drowning in the futility,

A scabbed sore is finally opened
on the endless journey of my healing.

_____

MEDIUMS

O N three separate occasions, I've had experiences with mediums who claimed to have messages for me from Erica. I didn't seek out any of these meetings. One was requested of me by the medium and that story is in the next section. Two happened unexpectedly while in conversation with two different women. I didn't realize either was a medium.

In 2006, I was attending a course on spirituality at a retreat centre in the Bronx in New York City. One of my friends in the program disappeared one afternoon and when I saw her later that day she told me she had received the most amazing foot massage from one of the participants and was feeling so euphoric she decided to go back to her room and relax rather than return to class. That sounded inviting to me.

At breakfast the next morning, I approached the massage therapist and asked if she had time to offer another foot massage. She did, and she did. As the massage was finishing, she asked if I had children. I told her I had two children, a young man, Colin, and a young woman, Erica. She asked me if one of them had passed away. I indicated Erica had died nearly six years earlier. She then told me that she was getting a message from Erica to let me know that all was well, and she was okay. I wasn't really ready for this conversation. I really hadn't thought much about mediums and while the experience brought tears, I wasn't totally convinced about what had just happened. It did, however, get my attention. Incidentally, in the course of that experience, she also channeled my father who indicated how proud he was of me and that he was very sorry for not having understood me for the person I was.

In the summer of 2010, I was at another workshop, this time at a retreat centre near our home in Caledon. During a break, I was walking outside on a beautiful day with another participant. I told her about Erica and moments later as we continued our walk she told me she had a message for me from Erica. I was surprised but not as startled as I had been in the previous meeting with the medium. She then went on to relate that Erica was now working with the souls of young people who had chosen to take their own lives and helping those souls to work through the pain that had caused them to take the action they had. Apparently, Erica exclaimed something like, "Isn't it amazing that I'm here doing work like you're doing there ... helping people grow and develop ... even though the reasons for the work might look different."

My attention was captured by these two experiences; I was curious and wanted to be open to whatever possibilities might exist. However, I didn't completely buy in to the medium experience. That view shifted with a third experience described in the next section.

Do Not Stand at My
Grave and Weep

ON a fall day in 2012, I received a phone call from a good friend to tell me that someone I had met a couple of years earlier was now referring to herself as a medium and that she was trying to get in touch with me because she had an important message. I hadn't particularly cared for that person when I'd met her before; however, I contacted her anyway. She told me I could speak with any medium and I'd get the message; however, she lived close by and we arranged a time for me to meet her the coming Saturday.

After getting comfortable in her quiet room, she proceeded to tell me that the message was from Erica who urgently wanted me to hear it and act on it. The medium began by telling me that Erica's spirit was in contact with and working with the spirit of a local doctor who had died a year earlier. They were working together helping with the healing of the spirits of deceased youth. I had never met the doctor; however, I was very familiar with his name. For the previous nine or ten months, I had been visiting with his wife as a volunteer with hospice, helping her process her grief.

The message from Erica was to exhort me to become much more active in helping other people understand that there was a form of existence following corporal death. The message went on to say that I was the right person to be spreading this message because of the many continuing experiences I'd had confirming that truth (i.e., those described herein).

She also joked that she had asked the doctor's spirit to be there with her in order to help me realize this was for real and the message ought to be taken seriously.

One of the things that struck me was the language and cadence of Erica's message; it sounded just like her.

When the session ended, I asked the medium whether she knew that I knew the doctor's wife. She claimed to not know that. I indicated I had to leave to get to a matinee stage performance in a nearby town. The medium told me that the doctor's wife and her sons (young men) would also be at that performance, after which the sons were coming for a session to connect them with the spirit of their father. The medium asked if I would return and also attend the session with the sons. The spirit of the doctor had indicated that he'd like me to be there. I said I wasn't sure about that — that at the very least I'd have to speak with their mother and with them to get their opinion and agreement.

As I drove home to pick up my wife and go to the play, I reflected that I still didn't really care for the personality of the medium and I wasn't totally clear what the medium might or might not have known in advance about Erica or my relationship with the late doctor's family. I was subsequently reminded by the medium's husband that I had earlier told Erica's story at a workshop that the two of them had led.

Sure enough, the mom and her sons were at the theatre and, during intermission, I spoke with the mom who confirmed they were going to the medium's home after the play. I asked her to ask her sons if they'd agree with my being there. They did.

At this session the primary "speaker" was the spirit of the doctor who asked his sons to use their talents in film production to create awareness in the world of the fact of life after death. He also said they ought to do that with me because I could bring practical business experience to the endeavour.

When the session ended I asked to spend a few minutes with the sons and asked them what they thought of what had just happened. They were intrigued but not certain of what it all meant. Unspoken, I suspect, was their own discomfort with the medium.

They were all staying for dinner; I left to have mine at home with my wife. As I began to drive toward the road, the radio was transmitting a weekly show, *Saturday Night Blues*, and the announcer was introducing the next song, the name of which I missed, by an artist I hadn't heard of, Harry Manx. As the gentle introduction led into a syncopated two-guitar blues-rock riff, I noted the appealing rhythm and sound. After close to a minute, the first lyrics began: *I am a thousand winds that blow*. Nice. A few lines later, *nice* transformed to *Oh my god*, as I listened to *Do not stand at my grave and cry/ I am not there, I did not die*. I knew these words and the complete lyrics. I had read them and spoken them many times. I knew them as part of a gentle reflective poem and yet here they were sung in a driving blues-rock format. The hair on the back of my neck was tingling and I found myself searching for breath as I cried and continued driving home up the country road.

What were the odds that that song, with that message, performed in that unexpected style, and on the radio station I was listening to at around 8 p.m. on a Saturday night, would play just as I got into the car, immediately following the experience described above. I remember thinking, *I might not care for the medium but this has got to be more than coincidence.* The message seemed crystal clear.

However, that's not all. For Erica's funeral, Roz created a lovely four-page service bulletin. On the front cover was a beautiful photo of Erica and a poem, and on the inside pages was the poem *The Dash*, as well as a song I wrote when Erica was born. The back cover had this poem:

Do not stand at my grave and weep,

For I am not there, I do not sleep.

I am a thousand winds that blow.

I am the diamond glints of snow.

I am the sunlight on ripened grain.

I am the gentle autumn's rain.

When you awake in the morning hush

I am the swift uplifting rush

Of quiet birds in circled flight.

I am the soft stars that shine at night.

Do not stand at my grave and cry;

I am not there, I did not die.

The order of the lines was changed in the sung version. There are many choral versions to be found on You Tube, but none remotely in the style played on the radio that night. You can follow this link to listen to Harry Manx's rendition: https://www.youtube.com/watch?v=-DxNS4WiyEI

The impact of this story has continued to resound, even in these moments of writing. While I'm moved by each of the experiences described here, this story above all holds my attention.

The back page of the service bulletin follows.

Do not stand by my grave and weep,
For I am not there, I do not sleep.
I am a thousand winds that blow.
I am the diamond glint of snow.
I am sunlight on ripened grain.
I am the gentle autumn's rain.
When you awake in the morning, hush.
For I am the swift uplifting rush
Of quiet birds in circle flight.
I am soft stars that shine at night.
Do not stand by my grave and cry.
I am not there, I did not die.

Erica's Tree:

Colin's Awakening

"Hey dad, what are you planning to do about Erica's tree?"

"What do you mean? I'm intending to leave it on the property."

"I've been getting messages from Erica that she's afraid of being left behind."

(with excitement and huge curiosity) "Let's talk!"

Out of the blue, completely unexpected and out of character, my son Colin was wondering what we were going to do about the lovely blue spruce that a group of special friends had purchased in memory of Erica a few weeks after her death, and which was planted in a corner of a horse paddock just beyond our log cabin.

Before moving to the subsequent conversation, let me share some background.

We'd been living on 28 acres of rolling farmland, which we'd reforested over the 25 years of living there. Erica loved that property, perhaps as much as Roz and I did — the open, unconstraining space, the peacefulness of nature's dominance, the regularity of seasonal cycles, the sacred intimacy with creation.

In the winter of 2014, after a couple of years of emotional preparation, Roz and I had decided to relocate our residence. We knew that the time would come at some point. What precipitated the decision was the realization that we wanted to spend as much time as possible with our grandchildren — Julian, five years old, and Lucy, three —before they grew up and became totally absorbed in their own lives. We began the purge and preparation ordeal in the spring, put the property on the market at the end of the summer, believing it would take at least until the following spring for a sale. The third couple to view the property put in an offer and purchased it, with a 30-day closing! The harrowing process of the next 30 days is an entirely separate story.

Some further background: In all the years following Erica's death, Colin had never raised the subject of Erica, or how he was feeling about her death or her life. Any time I tried to speak to him about her, my inquiry was met with some variation on, "I think about her every day. I don't need to talk about it."

We have a very loving relationship, so, while disappointed, I always assumed he'd talk about her if and when he was ready or had a need to.

Also, Colin had always appeared quite disinterested in my spiritual meanderings and I was okay with that, even though I wished it were different. Because of Colin's apparent attitudes, I was taken aback and highly intrigued to hear what he had experienced.

When we spoke, Colin told me that he'd had some experiences that left him convinced he wanted to have the memorial tree transplanted to his property in Collingwood.

First, he described a dream that he only remembered vaguely. He was in a forest, walking along a trail, when a large bird (?) flew overhead and down the trail where it went out of focus as it expanded in size. He awoke with a strong sense of Erica's presence, but nothing specific.

Second, he was at work one day taking his lunch break. Entering the staff lunchroom, he noticed a woman he didn't really know. His first instinct was to sit alone and re-energize for the afternoon. However, he chose to sit down beside her. After a few moments she turned to him and asked if he was aware that his sister was trying to reach him. Colin was certain there was little way this woman could even know he had a sister, alive or dead. He was shaken by this message coming so close on the heels of his dream.

Finally, he was getting a strong sense of a message that Erica was afraid of being *left behind* when we moved from the property in Caledon. Thus, his thinking that by taking the tree we would literally and figuratively be taking her with us. I hadn't considered that we were leaving Erica behind. She resides inside me spiritually and in memory, so the physical departure from the tree had no sense of leaving her behind any more than leaving the property itself did.

However, I then looked into the possibility of having the tree dug up, transported, and replanted. It could be done for $1,000. I was surprised at the low cost. However, when I thought about the limitation of the size of Colin's lot, it just didn't make sense to me. When we next spoke, Colin had come to the same conclusion.

A few days later, I was speaking with the woman who had purchased the property. We were standing outside the log house and discussing some issues around the paddocks they were planning on building and/or expanding. I asked her what she thought they'd do regarding the large blue spruce in the far corner of the paddock we were looking over. She responded; "It's such a gorgeous tree. We're planning on building a fence around it to protect it from the horses." My heart did a small leap and I told her about the significance of the tree. That led to tears and a reconfirmation of the intention to ensure the tree was protected, as well as an invitation to come back any time to be with the tree.

When I reflect on this story, it strikes me that all these years later, here I was about to make the same kind of under-estimation of the impact of distance and separation as I had made when I left Colin and Erica's mother back in the mid-'80s. It has caused me to reflect further on how it is I choose to be thoughtful and whether I thoroughly consider all points of view.

I'm left wondering about the messages Colin received. From where did they originate? How is it that pieces arise, sometimes repeatedly, and conjoin until there's a critical mass and the message is actually received? And, as always, with each of the stories related herein, what meaning can be teased out?

As result of this story, I began to be conscious in some way of Erica's presence most mornings as I walked the dogs at our new residence in Collingwood. The walk typically takes 45-60 minutes and often takes me along one of two piers that offer protection to the marina. As I would get to the end of the pier, I would begin singing a refrain: "Never left behind/ never left behind/ wherever now I travel/you're never left behind." Over time, lyrics began to form as I walked (much like the process that led to the creation of *I'm Thinking of You* several years earlier, back in Caledon). The full lyrics of the song follow.

Never Left Behind

Though your journey led to leaving
the place that we called home,
and you offered no forewarning
that you'd be forever gone,
there was built within our friendship
a love still growing strong
and it blossoms still, this morning
even though you've journeyed on.

Never left behind, never left behind
though life may call you to travel
no one's ever left behind
though our lives sometimes unravel
though the world can seem unkind
no one's ever left behind
no one's ever left behind.

When you were just a wee girl
I chose to leave your mom,
so caught up in my selfish needs,
sometimes weak then sometimes strong
and I only knew much later
through your anger and your tears
you'd lost your family not just your father
and my leaving drove your fears.

Never left behind, never left behind
though life may call you to travel
no one's ever left behind
though our lives sometimes unravel
though the world can seem unkind
no one's ever left behind
no one's ever left behind.

And our lives rewound together
our paths seemed clear and free
opportunities arising
some for you and some for me
When on a sunny summer morning
A knock came to the door
And the officer advised us
You'd be coming home no more.

Never left behind, never left behind
though life may call you to travel
no one's ever left behind
though our lives sometimes unravel
though the world can seem unkind
no one's ever left behind
no one's ever left behind.

Now it's once more time for leaving
This land that we've called home
Though my heart and soul seem rooted
In the earth and trees and stones
the land is just a certain place
the spirit knows no bounds
while my footsteps lead me onward
we'll forever know this ground.

Never left behind, never left behind
though life may call you to travel
no one's ever left behind
though our lives sometimes unravel
though the world can seem unkind
no one's ever left behind
no one's ever left behind …

you are never left behind
I am never left behind …

we are never left behind
we are never left behind.

————————————

Colin and Erica circa 1993

As the experience with the lyrics continued during the morning walks on the pier, I began to have intermittent experiences of another kind. Those are described in the story that follows.

SNOWY OWLS

IN my life, I had never seen a snowy owl. Of course, I hadn't expected to, because I assumed they lived year-round in the Arctic. In the summer of 2014, I was leaving Colin's home in Collingwood to return to Caledon. There on the rooftop of a house across the street was a large white owl that we subsequently determined was a snowy owl. What an awesome sight — at least two feet high and with a wingspan of almost five feet.

Circle forward to the weeks following our move to Collingwood. Walking the dogs along the pier at the marina, I saw another snowy owl. It was there intermittently for several weeks and then disappeared. It returned for a few days in the spring and then reappeared again in the fall of 2015 and then the winter of 2016, again intermittently, for a number of weeks.

There was another occasion — I was coming home after walking the dogs and a neighbour, Janelle, was outside our building staring up at the roof. There again was a snowy owl.

Finally, Roz and I were out walking the dogs in early January, in the dim pre-dawn light. A snowy owl was siting on a stump out in the bay, just offshore. It sat while we approached then flew to another roost and then continued down the bay and landed on the roof of another building and sat observantly until it flew again, this time out of sight. The close proximity and apparent comfort of the owl was thrilling.

In all, the sightings have perhaps numbered 20, at the time of writing. Where we live is within the winter migration territory of the snowy owl, so its presence certainly doesn't defy natural science. It's the persistent presence in the shadowy early morning light that gets my attention (quite aside from its absolute beauty). It's the time of day when my mind is quiet and I'm typically walking with heightened present-moment awareness. I'm enthralled by the conjunction of my readiness and the owls showing up.

According to the book *Animal Speak* by Ted Andrews, "Owls are the eyes of the night, and they can see what is not in the open." Because of the oversize of its wings relative to the size of its body and the fringe at the leading edge of its wings, the owl is able to fly silently and slowly. The possible learning is to cultivate silence as you go through life.

Because of the owl's association with the night, it is said to represent the holding and/or discovering of secrets. In some superstitions, the owl represents the reincarnation of the dead.

The snowy owl is both a diurnal and nocturnal creature. It hunts predominantly by sitting and waiting, conserving energy and observing constantly, and using a keen sense of timing to burst into action. It has a knack for moving to areas where food supplies will more likely be found and can instinctually detect possible famine periods. It has the power of prophecy and spirit.

The snowy owl does not proclaim its presence when it moves into a new area; it enters quietly. As Ted Andrews says, "When it walks, its talons are withdrawn into its well-padded feet ... reflecting its ability to be non-threatening in spite of its power and ability. It accomplishes its tasks with timing and skill, not through intimidation. True strength is gentle."

I have concluded that the snowy owl is my animal totem. In that respect it plays a role as teacher and mentor. That feels right to me.

Near-Death Experience
— My Story

ONE late afternoon, sometime in 2005, I was sharing a glass of wine with my mother who, at the time, would have been around the age of 85. Her physical mobility was compromised but her mind remained sharp, aware, and reflective. This get-together was pretty much a weekly ritual and generally a relaxed reflection on life memories (hers and mine), as well as stories of other family members and current events that she kept abreast of on CBC Radio.

At one point in the conversation, she made reference to "the time I dropped you down the stairs." My head jerked up and, as I stared at her, she could see the surprise on my face. "You know that story," she said. 'I've told you about that." I assured her that I didn't think I'd forget a story like that and I had absolutely no recollection of her ever telling me.

She elaborated:

"You were just an infant and you'd woken from a nap. After changing you, I wrapped you in a blanket and I was going to take you out into the back garden for some fresh air. As I reached for the door handle, you slipped out of my arms and fell down the basement stairs. When I got to the bottom of the stairs, you were unconscious. I picked you up, ran up the stairs, and then outside, hoping to find someone who could help get you to the doctor's office. Your father was at work with the only vehicle we owned. To my relief, there was a new neighbor moving in across the street and he drove us to the doctor's office. By the time we got there, you had regained consciousness. The doctor couldn't detect any serious injury and sent us home with instructions for me to monitor you. You remained fine and the incident passed … and well, just look at you now."

I don't know why my mother had never told me that story. However, in the wake of that revelation, I began to wonder if this might explain why I had felt, during my life, a comfort being with and/or talking about death and dying. By the time of this discussion, I had done much spiritual exploration. I had read about near-death experiences and now wondered if perhaps I had had one as a result of the fall. I had read about the soul entering a human life and shortly thereafter forgetting from what and from where it had come. I also recalled that people returning from near-death experiences are typically left with no fear of death.

I was left wondering if perhaps my infant subconscious or soul had somehow had a short-lived remembering of its origins. I also wondered if my comfort with death was born just shortly after my corporal birth through this experience.

That also makes me wonder whether having a near-death experience might explain why I've been so open to the events described herein.

I'm still wondering.

CONTEXT

I'VE been so profoundly and humbly blessed with the riches of my life. One of those blessings has been an inclination toward reflection. Though I try to live as much as possible in the present moment, and though I live with generally positive and upbeat anticipations for the future, I have consistently, over my life, spent time reflecting, assessing, and weaving a larger story out of the vignettes and passages of my days. Perhaps it has been my personal internalization of "the unexamined life isn't worth living" attributed by Plato to Socrates at his trial at which he chose death over exile. If so, that wasn't a conscious decision on my part.

Reflection has provided an opportunity to relive and re-experience events and circumstances of my life — sometimes with smiles and laughter, sometimes with tears and sadness, sometimes with anger and regret. It has also offered an opportunity to mull over and consider the context of those events and circumstances, to see how they might fit into a larger integrated context. For whatever reasons, I have a need for understanding and a curiosity about the notion of context.

One contextual focus has been cosmogenesis — the never-ending birthing and evolution of the universe. Another has been the rhythmical cycles of natural existence. I've come to appreciate the elegant nesting of the latter within the former so far as it relates to life and death. Theories about the beginning of the universe abound. For a while I was attracted to the notion that our universe arose out of a super supernova similar to the death of a star imploding into a black hole and subsequently re-emerging, only on a super-cosmic scale. This seemed to me to be also somehow related to the notion of a multiverse where the universe we know is only one of many.

However, I'm more comfortable now with the notion of a singular recycling universe; one that emerges from a singularity of energy (birth), a no-thing-ness, and expands (evolution) until it reaches some limit from which it then shrinks (devolution) until it returns to a singularity before the cycle is repeated.

It seems to me that this is a contextual reflection of what is continuously happening throughout the cosmos: birthing and dying of stars and solar systems and galaxies. That pattern is repeated in natural processes occurring on earth: mountain ranges form from the folding of the planetary crust and then over eons are smoothed by ice age glaciation and eroded by weather; trees are seeded, grow, and ultimately die into their base elements only to re-emerge in the cells of subsequently birthed vegetation.

Humans similarly are birthed, live, and die physically. The elements of the human body, whether buried or cremated or chewed on by charnel buzzards, are released into the earth or atmosphere, ultimately re-emerging.

The consistency of that general pattern throughout known physical existence reflects an elegance that appeals to me on a cognitive, and a creative, and a spiritual level. And it is not a demanding leap for me to consider the same might be happening on a dimension other than the physical. Indeed if, as it has been lyrically said, we are spiritual beings having a human experience, the profundity of the physical pattern might be minor relative to that of the spiritual.

As I began, I end: I have no idea how all of that might actually be. I do consider the possibility of existence beyond the physical and beyond the limits of time and space a valid subject matter for reflection. I don't understand what that reality might be like or why it might exist. And that's perfectly fine with me.

CONCLUSION

GIVE me mystery and give me wonder. That's enough, even in my reflecting on the being of Erica.

When you eventually see

through the veils to how things really are,

you will keep saying again and again,

This is certainly not like we thought it was!

— MEVLANA JALALUDDIN RUMI

———————

ACKNOWLEDGMENT

FROM the moment we learned about Erica's death, my wife Roz created and provided me with a loving container within which my grief could rise and abate in unpredictable waves of emotion. Additionally, prior to Erica's death, Roz had provided Erica with kindness, counsel, friendship and a loving acceptance as her stepmother. She remains angered by Erica's decision to get into her car and drive after the partying she had done. And she continues to love her.

APPENDIX 1

LIFE AFTER LIFE

IN his seminal work on near-death experiences, *Life After Life*, Raymond Moody reviews cases of near-death experiences his clients have shared with him. From these reflections, I have teased out the following common elements described as part of the experiences. There wasn't absolute commonality across all of the experiences but a compelling number of similarities to make a case that there might well be some other dimension of existence.

Here's an outline of those similarities.

- Hearing the news of one's death after dying and "never feeling so alive"

- Feelings of peace and quiet

- Hearing unusual noises

- Dark tunnel, tube, passageway

- Out of body experience, looking at the body

- Meeting others, both known (i.e., relatives) and unknown

- Seeing a being of light and experiencing unspoken communication; a sense of infinite compassion

- Life review … no judgment … non-sequential [everything comprehensively appearing at once] … implicit question, "How have you learned to love?"

- Reaching a border or limit from which you either pass over and remain dead or turn back to continue life

- Coming back

- Telling others about the experience but challenged by the inexpressibility

- Effect on life after — attitudes, choices, behaviours

- Relaxed attitude about death

- Life is about love not chasing after, it's about being and acceptance

- Life did not get easier following the experiences

Appendix 2

Here are the three poems that relate to the evolving experience of finding rabbit fur and blood in the snow on a sunny winter morning.

Living Blood Trilogy

Living Blood

It was the lingering vitality
The immanence of prehistoric struggle
That transformed the early moment,
Drawing a gasp for beauty
From the chapped lips of my soul.

Just beyond the beavered poplar
Gating progress along the trail
Emerged the vibrant living red
Against the receptive white of
Last night's crystalline snow.
Sanguine evidence,
Stark and soft,
Blood spattered,
Pollock-like
Beside random perfect pillowed tufts
Of beige and brown and gray and white.

An exquisite chaos
Releasing the waning, intertwined
Breathing of hunger and fear.
Testimony to the eternal dance
Of death and survival

Of giving and receiving
Of accepting and letting go,
Between consenting partners.
Each stepping to its own rhythm
Driven by its own heart drum
Melding in the one melody
Played in the primal key of Cosmos
Set in the sacred web of life.

Living Blood: Revisited

The image of blood and fur
Spiralled shallow and deep
Waters of my memory.

Days later
I freed myself to feel
The agony and the aching
The penetration of chiseled teeth
Tearing through fur and flesh;
To feel the terror of the hunted
To feel the hunger of the hunter.

Mouth opening in silent scream
Mouth closing in noisy appreciation.
Muscles tensing
Sinews snapping
Bones cracking
Warm blood spurting and flowing
In cavities of body and throat
The letting go letting go letting go ...
The spreading sense of satiation.
At a given instant
The loss of conscious participation
The losing of self in the unity of the dance.

One has walked away
The remains of one carried by the other
Into another instant.

I think I know a bit
About beginnings and endings.
And yet, I wonder,
In this encounter,
which was which …
which the sacrifice,
which the grace.

Living Blood: A Finally Opened Sore

I can hear your wild laughter
Bursting forth as you begin,
In the shadow of prudent travel,
The ill-advised adventure
To who knows where.

I can hear your gasp of incredulity
Brainstem flashing primordial warning
As the curve is missed
And you veer off the road
Into the dark void.

I can hear your scream!
I can hear your scream!
I can hear your scream!
I can hear your scream!

Piercing the seconds to eternity
As excitement crashes into chaos
As the car violently leaps and careens
Against and over the unseen boulders.

I can feel the smashing of hard metal
Against the softness of your defenceless body
Crushing and ripping your corporal being
Drenching the world in the blood of your living
The laws of physics and forces
Viciously declaring their truth

Strangling your laughter
Erasing your smile
Throwing you free of the mutilating machine
Throwing you free of the bonds of creation.

Oh God!
For so long I've avoided
This intimacy with your destruction.
For so long I've hidden out
In the metal-free meadows of illusion.
Swaddling myself in the beautiful memories
Wrapping my fear and ache in the tissue paper of spirit
Lacking the courage to really smell your fear
Lacking the courage to visit the imagined video
Lacking the courage to remove the earplugs from my heart
and really hear
and really hear
the horror
of your scream,
the mangling of metal
the grinding of rock
the tearing of grasses.

This day, in this visceral rawness
Of my unpackaged vulnerability,
Opened to the reality of your dying
Freed to the starkness of your fear
Choking for the loneliness of your suffering
Angry at your disregard of reality
Emptied of the meaning of your sacrifice
Closer to the scream in my heart
Sinking in the sadness
Drowning in the futility,

A scabbed sore is finally opened
On the endless journey of my healing.

———————————

Appendix 3

Other Selected Poems About Erica

Erica by Water

Tides of your presence
ebb and flow
through the murmuring seas
of my consciousness.

Waves of memory
break over my heart
healing again the leaking break
within.

Currents of time,
through inner and outer waters,
carry moments imagined and wanted
to the shores of my soul.

Pools of moonlight
reflect in rippled silence
the merging and emerging
of your spirit and the One.

Early autumn turnings
mark the past dry season
mimicking the desiccation
this passage leaves inside.

Last night's unexpected rain
bathes in greening mercy
the open and hidden landscapes
birthing tears and life anew.

Evening morning dew
moistens me and all
in drops of liquid clarity
quenching the grieving thirst.

Fall Fire

Like dry decaying bones of branches
pulled from the long bent grass
to blaze on the fall flames
with other bits of yesterday's green,
I call forth brittle memories of you
recalling the smile and laugh and hugs
that fired my heart with love
in the melt of swirling souls.

The light
the heat
the crackle
the char
the ash
the final wisps of smoke ...

one fire
one life.

August 30th

The morning dew hangs heavy
drops on the stalks of tall grass
and intricate spider works between
leaning in the spa0rkling blue sky air.

My foot falls slow and heavy
as morning trail-walking ritual
with the canine daughters
is shrouded in memories of this date.

Eight years and eternity has passed
since the ominous informing arrival
of a uniform at the door, gently
announcing the accident
and the death.

Tears fall in the shade of the memorial spruce
and are licked amid the echoing sobs
by Annie's curious concern
and Maya's loving presence ...
and I sing my grieving song.

The afternoon sun shines restoratively
as the memories ebb and flow
while I flow toward the celebration
of another more recent daughter's birth.

And then I'm watching Julian ...
rolling over, stretching for propulsion
my mouth stretches with his smiles
and I feed apple sauce into his
seven month old descendant life.

He pulls the glasses from my face
infant discovery opens my eyes
outpouring of caring and joy
floods the temporarily desiccated
plains of my heart.

Later, under the stellar abyss
my being oscillates
on the scales of emotion ...
love in its many weights
realigns and realigns
the vital balance.

_____

The Sweetness that Follows the Grief

Cold steel
chisels the rock …
fragments fall under my feet …
bleeding naked soles
grease the tunnel
of the deepest dark.

Blueberry juices
cascade from my eyes
and drop by drop
slowly bathe
my taste buds alive
with the sweetness
that follows the grief.

Your Smile

When my mind intercepts a glimpse of memory

it's your smile that emerges through the haze of time,

the smile that brightened the rooms of my joy, and

the one that undid me in moments of anger.

These days I'm hard-pressed to be sure whether

it's in fact your smile or a photo-captured image

that forms when I seek the sense of your presence.

And then, smiling, I let go of the effort to recall, and

open the window of my heart to the heart of your essence

and I feel it in the depths of my loving and my loss,

no need to bring it to the screening of my mind's eye

for it floods the dry plain of my grieving and

lights even the darkest recesses of my unrequited yearning.

_____

ABOUT THE AUTHOR

After a career in business, including over 20 years as president and/ or CEO of several companies in Canada, Jake McArthur has created a meaningful palette of purposeful engagements in the world, including executive coaching, group facilitation, and leadership workshops with adults and with elementary school children. For many years, he has written and performed poetry. He has written short plays, three of which have been performed in local amateur theatre, and he has acted on stage with both amateur and professional companies.

For twenty years, Jake was an avid volunteer with various hospice organizations. Today he also serves as a registered celebrant for weddings and end-of-life celebrations.

In support of his evolution through the chapters of his living, he has obtained a BA, an MBA, and a Doctor of Ministry.

He lives with Roz, his wife of over 30 years, and a dog or two, in Collingwood, Ontario, Canada. He is blessed that his son Colin, an osteopath, lives close by in Collingwood with his wife Lisa and their four delicious children — Julian, Lucy, Devon, and Travis, as does Violet, mother of Julian and Lucy.

Opening to the Mystery
Live Performance

JAKE has created and performs a stage production of *Opening to the Mystery*. He welcomes opportunities to share the spoken word version of the stories and poems from this book.

He can be contacted at jakecelebrant@icloud.com.

Audience members have reflected:

Thank you for an outstanding evening of theatre. You nailed it. Your performance was honest, direct and courageous. Erica would be even more proud of her old man. You brought tears to my old eyes. You were terrific. Your voice and your pacing, your humour and your authenticity all shone through. — BW

I really enjoyed your performance of Opening to the Mystery. *I loved hearing your stories and listening to the sounds and feeling all of the emotions. It was obvious that the audience was totally enraptured with your message! Wow! I was very impressed. The Q and A was a nice addition and folks had some really good thoughts to share.* — LM

You were brilliant, inspiring, illuminating, stately and humble. — LH

You are truly a great performer and storyteller ... both of which I suspect are easy to do with such a personal topic. Clearly you spoke from the heart and while continuing your emotional healing, it allowed the audience, starting with me, things to think about. — FS

I want to tell you how much I enjoyed your show last night. It was powerful and moving — and empowering, too, in your honesty and openness to grief and loss and possibility. The poetry of the canoe and butterfly sequence is breathtaking. I was mesmerized by that scene in particular. — JW

I don't know if you could feel the people in the room from the stage but the impact of your stories, and the loving reception of them was palatable. You deeply affected all those who were present. — SF

www.ingramcontent.com/pod-product-compliance
Lightning Source LLC
Chambersburg PA
CBHW041540120626
46551CB00019B/2772